Impressionism

Impressionism

John Russell Taylor

IVY LEAF

Contents

HALF-TITLE PAGE Pierre-Auguste Renoir
The box at the theatre (1874)
London: Courtauld Institute Galleries

TITLE SPREAD Camille Pissarro
The Crystal Palace, London (1871)
Chicago: Art Institute

THIS SPREAD Édouard Manet
Road-menders in the rue de Berne (1877–8)
London: National Gallery (Lady Butler Loan)

First published in Great Britain in 1981 by
Octopus Books Limited

This edition published in 1990 by
Ivy Leaf
Michelin House
81 Fulham Road
London SW3 6RB

© 1981 Octopus Books Limited

ISBN 0 86363 013 8

Printed in Hong Kong

Antecedents

By the 1850s, when most of the artists who were eventually to be known as Impressionists had their first contacts with the Paris art world, art in France had settled into a rut. For any would-be artist, progress toward official recognition involved submission to the art establishment, which ordained that you could not do this before you had done that, that you had to have attended the right school (the École des Beaux-Arts) or have been the pupil of one of the right painters, and above all that you had to have the approval of the ultimate authority, the Academy of Fine Arts, and exhibit at the Academy's biennial Salon before anyone would take you seriously and buy your work.

The Academy was at this time dominated by the great Neo-Classical painter Ingres, who insisted that everyone must more or less follow his example, with its strong emphasis on the formal organization of a picture and on traditional draughtsmanship learnt in the wearisome school of copying the masters and drawing objects and human models with a hard, clear line. A career in art, while not wholly impossible, could prove extremely difficult for painters who would not follow this line and submit to the ideas of the Academy. Ingres's great rival Delacroix, the type of the fiery, Romantic painter, replaced the cool repose of Ingres's canvases with tempestuous scenes of passion and drama painted in a free, improvisatory way to match his subjects. His work was rejected time and again by the Academy, but he persisted with his attempts to get in, since it was the only certain way to advancement. Other great non-conformists of the time were also shunned: Gustave Courbet, the master of realism, had two important pictures rejected from the official French show of art at the 1855 Exposition Universelle in Paris.

It was a lot for young artists, still students or just starting out on their careers, to rebel against. And none of the Impressionists-to-be started in revolt against the academic establishment. Indeed, most of them may be said to have fought as long as possible against being rebels, and to have given in to the idea of rebellion only when there seemed to be no other way. The most mature of them, Édouard Manet, came of a prosperous Paris family and sought worldly success in the conventional way, studying under one of the Beaux-Arts painter-instructors, Thomas Couture, for six years and aiming directly at success in the Salon, which in 1861 he achieved with his *Spanish guitar player*. Camille Pissarro, after a childhood in the West Indies, enrolled at the Beaux-Arts and at the same time sought advice from Corot, a sensitive painter of atmospheric landscapes and one of the less controversial among the leading 'outsiders'. Edgar Degas, a young man-about-town of similar background to Manet's, two years younger and soon to be a close friend of his, enrolled in the Beaux-Arts in 1855, and carefully shunned any association with the 'unwashed' bohemian members of the artistic fraternity.

The establishment, however, seemed bent on laying up trouble for itself. In 1859, the year the precocious 19-year-old Claude Monet arrived in Paris from Le Havre, the Salon rejected important pictures by Manet, the flower-painter Henri Fantin-Latour, and the eccentric young American James McNeill Whistler. The rejected paintings were promptly exhibited in a private studio, and created a stir. The following year the idea was pursued again, with a large-scale show of painters on the fringes of or outside the Academy, including Delacroix, Courbet, Corot, and Millet and other landscape painters working around Barbizon (near Fontainebleau), who had made a principle of painting in the open air. In 1861 Pissarro met a rough-mannered young Provençal, Paul Cézanne, at a

Jean-Baptiste-Camille Corot
(1796–1875)
Sainte-Cathérine-lez-Arras
1872–3
Oil on canvas
59 × 43.5 cm (23¼ × 17⅛ in)
Texas: private collection

Although in many respects Corot was, in his approach to landscape painting, nearer to the classical Poussin of two centuries earlier than to anything in his own time, he was also an important precursor of the Impressionists, above all in his fascination with light and its effects. He liked to paint his subjects from nature, and as he progressed he became less interested in rendering landscape with 'scientific' objectivity and more in capturing an immediate visual experience of it. This is one of his last paintings; it was apparently begun on the spot and completed in his studio, and it was finished only a year before the first Impressionist show. The way the trees are painted, in particular, shows how objectively recorded botanical detail has given way to a delicate 'impression' of how they look. This would have been much to the Impressionists' taste, even if they would not quite have approved of Corot's artificially limiting his colours to a narrow range of grey-greens.

private school called the Académie Suisse, where poor painters could paint from live models at little expense. In 1862 Monet, after a period of military service, returned to Paris and, in order to placate his family, enrolled in the studio of one of the Beaux-Arts painters, Charles Gleyre, where he met three other new students: Frédéric Bazille, like Cézanne a southerner of comfortable bourgeois background; Pierre-Auguste Renoir, who had managed to earn enough money for his training from painting porcelain in a factory; and Alfred Sisley, who was of British origin although born and brought up in Paris.

Thus by 1862 all the principal figures in Impressionism were already assembled in Paris, and most of them were known, at least remotely, to one another. The only one who had in any way the temperament of a rebel was Monet, who constantly expressed impatience with academic methods and disciplines. All the rest, whatever their respect for the great outsiders such as Courbet, Corot, and even Delacroix (finally elected to the Academy in 1857), seemed set on conventional academic careers. But 1863 brought an important change in the Paris art scene: that year the selection committee for the Salon rejected so many works that a direct appeal was made to the Emperor; he responded by setting up a Salon des Refusés (to open two weeks after the official Salon), in which any painter whose work had been rejected could, if he chose, exhibit within a stone's throw of the Salon itself. Manet found himself among these with his *Luncheon on the grass*, rejected by the Salon and found 'immodest' by the Emperor himself. He showed it among the refused pictures, and it created a scandal – although not at this point a very profitable one. The lesson had been learnt by the Academy, however, and the following year (1864) Manet was back in the Salon with another now-famous painting, *Olympia*. Showing alongside him were Degas, Pissarro, Renoir, Berthe Morisot, and even Monet, whose sea and river scenes were very favourably received.

During the next six years or so, the selectors for the Salon followed a zigzag course, sometimes leaning towards liberalism, sometimes towards ultra-conservatism, while the critics supported now one side, now another. Although more and more voices were heard in favour of the new painters and their new approaches to colour and form, in popular estimation the Salons remained the ultimate authority. Clearly something had to be done to bring about a shift in taste. Manet, once he had become convinced that there was no longer any hope in the Salon, came to look more and more like the leader of a new movement, whose members soon became known as *la bande à Manet* (Manet's gang). By the end of the decade almost all the Impressionists had got into the habit of meeting, whenever they happened to be in Paris, at the Café Guerbois (in what is now Avenue de Clichy) to pass agreeable social evenings and talk, sometimes with passion, about art and society. The Franco-Prussian War of 1870, the succeeding siege of Paris, and the short-lived Commune which governed it between the fall of the Second Empire and the establishment of the Third Republic, drastically broke into the apparently measured, immutable progress of the Academy and the Salons. And when the scattered painters returned to Paris (minus Bazille, who had been killed in the war) they were convinced that it was time to make a new start.

Gustave Courbet (1819–77)
Immensity
1869
Oil on canvas
60×82.2 cm ($25\frac{5}{8} \times 32\frac{3}{8}$ in)
London: Victoria and Albert
Museum

Courbet was famous (or notorious)
in his time for his supposedly
ruthless realism, which in most of
his critics' minds, and perhaps his
own, was bound up with his very
left-wing politics. He certainly
painted scenes of contemporary
working-class life; and when he
worked in traditional Salon genres,
such as the nude, he did it in a very
different, 'unclassical' way, his
models being entirely unidealised.
Later in life his work began to take
on a symbolic quality, a result of the
load of social significance he wanted
it to carry. There was much about
his painting the Impressionists could
not approve, although they
applauded his rebellious spirit. But
his landscapes and seascapes were
an exception: here his insistence on
painting just what was there before
him accorded very well with their
own views, even if Courbet saw it in
rather a different way. And his great
vistas of sky, such as *Immensity*, are
among the first creations of pure
atmosphere in French art.

Édouard Manet (1832–83)
Luncheon on the grass
1863
Oil on canvas
208 × 265 cm (84¼ × 106¼ in)
Paris: Louvre (Jeu de Paume)

This painting was the great
sensation of the Salon des Refusés
in 1863. It was one of three
paintings that Manet included, and
was originally entitled *Le bain* (The
bath). It owed its notoriety partly at
least to the Emperor's known
opinion that it was 'immodest',
which naturally brought in the
crowds. The immodesty consisted
largely of placing nude or semi-nude
women in the same picture with
fully dressed men – and men,
moreover, wearing contemporary
French clothes rather than
something discreetly 'period' or
mythological. Manet came in for the
same sort of criticism as had
Courbet before him: his painting
was 'vulgar', lacking that saving
touch of the 'ideal' which removed
Salon nudes from base modern
reality. A leading critic of the day,
while admitting that Giorgione had
done the same thing, concluded that
'the nude, when painted by vulgar
men, is inevitably indecent'. In all
the flurry, no one noticed Manet's
strong fresh colour or the skill with
which he painted light filtering
through leaves.

Pierre-Auguste Renoir (1841–1919)
La Grenouillère
1869
Oil on canvas
50 × 57 cm (19½ × 22½ in)
Stockholm: Nationalmuseum

In 1868–9 Renoir and Claude Monet
spent a lot of time together on the
Seine near Bougival, a few miles
downriver from Paris, where La
Grenouillère (The Frogpond) was a
popular place of resort in the
summer with its restaurant, bathing,
and boating (both painters were
enthusiastic oarsmen). At this time
they were having no success at all in
the art market, and Monet was so
poor he often could not afford to
buy paints. But somehow a lot of
work got done, often with the two
artists painting the same subject
from almost exactly the same angle,
as in the case of this view. Like the
other true Impressionists, they
painted very quickly – and in a way
the Salon painters would consider
shamelessly sketchy and unfinished
– to capture the life and movement
of the holiday-makers, the ever-
shifting patterns of light and shade,
and above all the effect of water,
which in this painting catches
colour from its surroundings and
throws back reflected light in a way
that was then completely new to art.

The Heyday of Impressionism

What did the young painters talk about in those formative years at the Café Guerbois? No precise account seems to have survived, although there are many testimonials to the tonic effects the Thursday night get-togethers had on the participants. They must have been a curious assortment – the rather grand Parisians Manet and Degas, for instance, rubbing shoulders with the working-class Renoir and the aggressively provincial Cézanne. Nor were their politics any more consistent than their backgrounds. The gentle Pissarro, son of a Jewish-French shop-keeper, was at heart a fiery anarchist; Monet, whose father was a ship's chandler, was almost as far left of centre, as well as being an uncompromising revolutionary in artistic matters; Manet, on the contrary, inclined to political conservatism. Berthe Morisot, a grand-daughter of the painter Fragonard and a former pupil of Corot, came from an aristocratic family. Sisley, born into the professional classes, had been earmarked by his father for a business career. Degas, something of a cool, ironical dandy in every area of his life, insisted on infuriating everyone else by adopting a lofty, patrician view of art and its public; sometimes he defended the most reactionary of the establishment painters on the grounds of their confident craftsmanship and their ability to do to perfection what they set out to do, however objectionable their artistic aims might be.

In other words, the Café Guerbois set, before and after the Franco-Prussian War, was a bunch of artists linked together by personal friendship and passionate involvement in the matter of art, rather than a narrowly doctrinaire group with a coherent and easily definable programme for changing the world. The big thing they had in their favour was their talent and their concern for the cause of art. And for all their personal differences they had, fundamentally, quite a lot in common. They were very much of an age: in 1870 Pissarro was 40, Manet 38, Degas 36, Cézanne and Sisley 31, Monet 30, and Renoir and Morisot 29. They were all relatively outsiders in the art world, since only Manet had up to then had anything like a critical success, let alone a commercial one. And on a deeper level they were all, at this formative period in their careers, going in much the same direction and were thinking about art in much the same way.

The great battleground among the academics, at the time when they were first feeling their way as artists, had been between the proponents of 'line' (Ingres and his followers) and the proponents of 'colour' (Delacroix and his group). Ingres held that the basis of painting was drawing: first you got all the outlines down in detail and in their proper place, then you painted them in decorously, in subdued and harmonious colours, with as perfect a finish as possible, eliminating all evidence of individual brushstrokes and other physical processes of painting. Delacroix, on the other hand, believed that much of what was important about painting resided in the very process of painting, and that hard outlines counted for little: forms in painting were built up from individual brushstrokes, and the dramatic use of colour was paramount.

In this argument the Impressionists were wholeheartedly with Dela-croix, but they carried his ideas several stages farther. They recognised that colour is a property of light, and that form is also created and modified by the play of light. Although they did not at this stage theorise very much about such matters (that was to come with a later generation), they were artistically fascinated, for instance, by snow and the way it reflects light and by water and the way its ripples break up light. They

Édouard Manet
Eva Gonzalez
1870
Oil on canvas
198 × 135 cm (78 × 53⅛ in)
London: National Gallery

In spite of the spectacular showing he had made in the Salon des Refusés, Manet continued to aim at the official recognition of the Salons, and among the pictures he painted each year would be a few intended for submission to the Salon. His portrait of *Eva Gonzalez* is one of these: a large picture, about two metres high, it shows one of Manet's pupils posed at her easel painting a vase of flowers. Unlike many of the portraits Manet was painting about this time, principally of his family and friends, there is something rather stiff and formal about the composition. Manet often took the hint for his compositions from the old masters (even *Luncheon on the grass* is based on a drawing by Raphael), and here he seems to be deliberately harking back to an 18th-century tradition of (usually) self-portraiture. He had a lot of trouble with this painting, needing more than 40 sittings, and the white muslin of the dress is much more vividly rendered than the character of the sitter.

therefore had great areas of subject-matter in common, and would frequently paint the same scenes side by side – Monet and Renoir at La Grenouillère in Croissy, Sisley and Monet at Argenteuil, Pissarro and Cézanne at Pontoise; all three locations were dominated by rivers. They had also become aware of the development of photography, and the way that the camera's eye sees objects modified by light in ways that the human viewer, his vision 'refined' or 'edited' by knowledge of the objective shape of such objects, does not normally perceive. This new visual evidence influenced the way they painted – particularly in the case of Degas.

When the friends reassembled in Paris towards the end of 1871, after scattering to the provinces or foreign parts during the war and the subsequent troubles, they were very much of one mind on the desirability, if not the absolute necessity, of painting on the spot, and capturing the precise effects of light at a particular instant in time. (Only Degas tended in the opposite direction, preferring to sketch, or merely to observe, his favourite back-stage scenes at the Opéra and then to paint them from memory and imagination in the studio.) No one knew how the official art world of the new republic would shape, and while everyone was waiting to see whether the Salon of 1872 would be significantly different from those of the defunct Empire, the group met someone who was going to be important in their later careers, the dealer Paul Durand-Ruel. He had a gallery in London, and in 1870 Pissarro had met and received much encouragement from him there. Back in France Durand-Ruel bought Sisleys and Degas, and then, early in 1872, a considerable number of Manets. These painters and others of the group were strongly represented in his London exhibitions of 1872, 1873, and 1874.

Most of them did not try to put anything into the Salon of 1872, perhaps out of some kind of loyalty to Durand-Ruel. In any case, this was probably just as well because the Salon proved if anything more conservative than before. Protests followed, and were intensified in 1873, only to be partially met by the organization of another Salon des Refusés, this time called an Exposition Artistique des Oeuvres Refusées. Oddly enough, that year Manet again had a considerable success within the Salon, particularly with an old-masterly portrait called Le bon bock, which most of his painter friends found disappointingly conformist; Renoir was one of the most successful in what proved to be a very well received show of the rejected. But it was becoming evident that things could not go on like this. And with even Durand-Ruel having to cut down purchases because of an economic recession, it looked as though the non-conformist painters would have to help themselves.

Thus was born the idea of putting on a show of their own. Monet, ever the rebel, seems to have been the one to push the idea through, and the more practical and diplomatic Pissarro the one who did most of the detailed organising. It was decided that there should be a sort of joint-stock company to which each of the participating artists would contribute equally. The placing of individual pictures would be determined first of all by size, then by drawing lots. The document which made it official was dated 27 December 1873. Among the founder-members were Monet, Pissarro, Degas (although he expressed doubts about making it too narrowly based), Renoir, Sisley, and Berthe Morisot. They soon acquired premises, thanks to the kindness of the photographer Nadar (Félix Tournachon), who allowed them to use free of charge the studios he had just vacated off the Boulevard des Capucines. Various other artists were persuaded to join in, among them some older, more established figures such as Eugène Boudin and the etcher Félix Bracquemond, and in all 165 works by 30 artists were assembled. The show opened on 15 April 1874, for one month. Of the major Impressionists, only Manet refused to take part, persisting in his view that a separate show was wrong, that the battle should be joined and won in the Salon; indeed, he was not to exhibit at any of the Impressionists' shows.

In most practical terms the show was a disaster. It was reviewed savagely or jocularly in the press, the most notorious piece coming from a

Édouard Manet
Nana
1877
Oil on canvas
150 × 116 cm (59 × 45⅝ in)
Hamburg: Kunsthalle

Among Manet's close friends was the realist novelist Emile Zola, who in 1876 had caused a stir with *L'assommoir*, his shocking novel of Parisian lowlife. The central character of this story is the mother of a little girl called Nana, who was to emerge in Zola's next novel as a highly successful kept woman. In his painting *Nana* Manet frankly depicts such a character, in her underclothes, powdering herself in front of a mirror, while a formally dressed man in a top hat watches her from the edge of the frame. The situation is hardly one of cosy domesticity, and spectators could be left in little doubt that this is a *demi-mondaine* and her keeper – especially since it was an open secret that the model had been the well-known mistress of a foreign prince. The painting was rejected by the Salon, and it later created a scandal when exhibited in the window of a fashionable art gallery.

Édouard Manet
Claude Monet in his studio-boat
1874
Oil on canvas
81 × 104 cm (32 × 41 in)
Munich: Neue Pinakothek

Partly no doubt because he was
more interested in the old masters
than the other Impressionists and
took a more traditional view of the
painter's role in society, Manet was
slow to take up the idea of painting
on the spot, in the open air. But in
the summer of 1874 all that changed
quite dramatically when he spent
some time painting with Monet and
Renoir at Argenteuil, a small town
just down-river from Paris. There it
was Monet's convictions which
especially affected him, and although
he never became particularly
interested in landscape as such, he
took to painting people out of doors.
Paintings like *Claude Monet in his
studio-boat* have a new freedom in
their treatment, using smaller, more
sketchy strokes and a brighter range
of colours, and picking up in typical
Impressionist fashion the light
reflected from water and the almost
abstract play of colours broken up
by the ripples.

Édouard Manet
The Grand Canal, Venice
1875
Oil on canvas
57 × 48 cm ($22\frac{1}{2}$ × $18\frac{7}{8}$ in)
San Francisco: private collection

The following year Manet visited
Venice in the company of James
Tissot, a painter friend from outside
the Impressionist circle (although in
his fascination with society and the
dress and bearing of beautiful
women and handsome men Tissot
was not always remote from Manet
himself). In spite of Tissot's
company, Manet painted, in *The
Grand Canal, Venice*, one of his
most dashingly Impressionist works,
in which the dazzling Italian
sunlight reduces the architecture in
the background to a golden-pink
blur of shapes barely indicated, and
the pale blue of the sky becomes a
richer, deeper blue when reflected in
the waters of the canal. For all its
apparent speed of execution,
however, it is an unusually intricate
composition, with the play of near
and far emphasized by the placing
of the boldly striped poles receding
just right of centre and the gondolas
on either side brusquely chopped off
by the picture's frame.

16

critic called Louis Leroy of *Le Charivari*, whose only claim to fame is that, in heading his article 'Exhibition of the Impressionists' (the term was borrowed from the title of one of Monet's paintings – see page 29), he accidentally created the label which would stick; used at first in derision by enemies, the term was then adopted with pride by the group. Not many paintings were sold that year, and those which were brought rather low prices. When the time came for accounting at the end of the year, the society was found to be in debt, and a move to dissolve it at once was unanimously accepted. So it seemed as though the brave enterprise had come to an ignominious end. But the ties of friendship remained strong, and in the months following the show the Impressionist 'line' became even clearer. Monet and Renoir spent a lot of time with Manet at Argenteuil, and by their example finally converted him completely to open-air painting. And the group created another scandal when in 1875 Monet, Renoir, Sisley, and Morisot arranged for an auction sale of their works (73 altogether) to take place at the Hôtel Drouot in Paris. The scene here was so disorderly, and the prices fetched so derisory, that they put off plans for a new group show until 1876.

The second show had taken place in April 1875 in Durand-Ruel's galleries, and if the attitudes of the press seemed to have changed little at least the show did not make a loss; some of the paintings (such as Monet's *Japonnerie*, a portrait of a young woman in a kimono) sold for relatively high prices, and word of this new movement in French art (although not always very favourable word) had started to spread abroad. The Impressionists had also acquired a lifelong patron and enthusiast, Victor Chocquet, who had a special admiration for Cézanne but also bought works by the others and tirelessly publicised them. Another wealthy friend and patron, Gustave Caillebotte (who had been a neighbour of the Manet group at Argenteuil), was by profession an engineer but was also an amateur painter of no mean talent. He brought his considerable organizing abilities to bear on the problem of the next group show, which was located in the same street as Durand-Ruel's gallery, was officially called the Exposition des Impressionistes, and for the first time had built into its rules the condition that exhibitors could not also exhibit in the Salon. This was in April 1877. Despite, or because of, the firm stand, the reception was little more favourable than before. But the tide was turning. In 1879 the fourth group show (tactfully dropping the word 'Impressionist' from its title) had a modest financial success and even some unreserved praise in the press. Renoir, Sisley, and Cézanne were not included for various practical reasons and Berthe Morisot was pregnant; but there were additions to the group, the most notable being the American Mary Cassatt.

The friends, however, were already beginning to go in different directions. Degas was the centre of a lot of quarrels. Monet dropped out of the fifth exhibition (1880), although Paul Gauguin appeared there, as a pupil of Pissarro. Caillebotte dropped out of the sixth show in 1881, and by this time Monet, Renoir, Cézanne, and Sisley had gone back to submitting (with variable success) to the Salon. In 1882, owing to the diplomacy of Caillebotte and the businesslike determination of Durand-Ruel, the seventh show reunited all the major Impressionists except Degas (and of course Manet, who had never exhibited with them). Although the general public remained indifferent or hostile, they were becoming almost an accepted group within the French art establishment. In 1882 Manet, after exhibiting *A bar at the Folies-Bergère* in the Salon, was finally awarded the Légion d'Honneur, although he did not live to enjoy the distinction for very long. It was really the end of Impressionism as well as its consecration. By the time of the eighth and last show in 1886, nearly all the originators had fallen away except Degas and Pissarro (who was painting in quite a new style), while other, very different artists took part and attracted most of the attention: Gauguin again, but also Georges Seurat, Paul Signac, Pissarro's son Lucien, and even the Symbolist Odilon Redon. Impressionism was giving way to Post-Impressionism, and a new era was dawning.

Édouard Manet
A bar at the Folies-Bergère
1882
Oil on canvas
96 × 130 cm (37¾ × 51¼ in)
London: Courtauld Institute
Galleries

Manet's last major painting, this was
in fact painted in 1881, but it was
dated 1882 and was first shown in
the Salon of that year. Manet was

now becoming crippled by the
disease (locomotor ataxia) that
would kill him the following year,
and henceforward he would be
unable to work on anything more
ambitious than small-scale pastels
and water-colours. By the Salon of
1882 he had finally earned complete
acceptance by the art establishment
and he was to be made a Chevalier
of the Légion d'Honneur just after
the Salon closed. But his work was

still not fully understood: spectators
attuned to the story-telling art of the
usual Salon painter paid much more
attention to the subject-matter of his
paintings than to their technique (as
they had earlier with *Luncheon on
the grass* and *Nana*). The virtuosity
with which lights and reflections are
handled, and with which the textures
of glass and marble and fabric and
fruit are differentiated, escaped
contemporary critics entirely.

Edgar Degas (1834–1917)
The ballet scene from Meyerbeer's 'Robert-le-diable'
1876
Oil on canvas
75×81 cm ($29\frac{1}{2} \times 31\frac{7}{8}$ in)
London: Victoria and Albert Museum

Unlike the other Impressionists (with the partial exception of Manet), Degas was never much interested in landscape and painting in the open air; nor was he greatly concerned with another Impressionist preoccupation, capturing the fleeting moment. He particularly relished the atmosphere of theatres and bars and brothels, the strange effects of artificial light, and the odd compositions suggested by the viewpoint of the audience or the privileged spectator from the wings in a theatre. In 1868 he became friendly with a bassoonist in the orchestra of the Paris Opéra and did a number of paintings showing the orchestra in the pit and a performance in progress on-stage in the background above them. This is the most famous of these paintings. Degas had first painted the subject in 1872, introducing into the foreground as members of the audience several recognisable portraits of friends and acquaintances, such as the banker-patron Albert Hecht. The picture was bought at once by Durand-Ruel, who showed it in London that winter. Four years later Degas painted this version, very much the same but with the figures at the front rearranged.

Edgar Degas
The dancing class
1875
Oil on canvas
85 × 75 cm ($33\frac{1}{2}$ × $29\frac{1}{2}$ in)
Paris: Louvre

Another aspect of Degas' interest in
the theatre shows in his series on
the theme of the ballet-girl. Although
in the later 19th century there was a
sort of aesthetic and intellectual cult
of the ballet-girl and her humbler
sister the chorus-girl, Degas seems to
have had no such fancy ideas about
them; he was fascinated by the
movements of the dancers and the
changing shapes of their costumes
in different lights and from different
angles. Degas rarely painted on
the spot, but later in his career he
favoured rapid media such as pastel
for catching the effects of theatrical
lighting in all its richness. This oil
painting of 1875 is one of his earlier
and more conventional treatments of
the subject: the composition seems to
have been very carefully considered,
the dancer on the piano being a late
addition.

Edgar Degas
Miss La La at the Cirque Fernando
1879
Oil on canvas
117 × 77.5 cm (46 × 30½ in)
London: National Gallery

Allied to the theatrical themes in
Degas's work were treatments of the
circus world. Miss La La, billed as
the 'woman-cannon', was a mulatto
performer whose speciality was feats
of strength performed with her teeth.
In January 1879 she was performing
at the Cirque Fernando in Paris,
where Degas saw her on at least
four occasions and made copious
sketches and notes of her poses and
of the architectural setting. He then
did a large-scale sketch in oil and
distemper of La La performing this
feat, in which she was lifted up to
the roof by her teeth. Finally he did
the painting as we know it,
conveying the precariousness of the
lift entirely by the dizzying angle
from which the view is taken. This
was one of his most calculated
works, based on complementary
colours (orange and blue in the
building, yellow and lilac in the
costume), and intended to shock;
oddly, it went almost unremarked in
the fourth Impressionist show.

Edgar Degas
The beach
1876
Oil on paper mounted on canvas
47 × 82.5 cm (18½ × 32½ in)
London: National Gallery

In this work Degas seems for a moment to have shared the fascination of his fellow Impressionists with the cool, clear light and the pale colours of water and sand on the Channel coast of France. But the concentration on people rather than setting, and the humanly intimate moment of a mother dressing her daughter's hair, are more typical of Degas's usual interests as a painter. The artful and intricate composition, with clothes and parasol laid out, lower right, as a sort of abstract pattern pulling our attention provocatively off-centre, suggests the influence of Japanese prints, which Degas was studying at the time – and perhaps also the curiously arbitrary 'cut-off' effects of early snapshot photographs. Degas certainly used photographs as the basis of some of his compositions. This was probably not one of them, but it seems unlikely to have been painted on the spot, as Impressionist principle would have had it: no doubt it was carefully constructed in Degas's studio from sketches.

22

Camille Pissarro (1830–1903)
The Louveciennes road
1870
Oil on canvas
60 × 73 cm (23⅝ × 28¾ in)
Paris: Louvre (Jeu de Paume)

Early in his career Pissarro was in
general the most sober and slow-
moving of all the major
Impressionists. On his arrival in
France in 1855 from his home in the
West Indies he had been especially
impressed by the landscapes of
Corot and Courbet, and he began to
work his way towards an individual
style by means of painting dark-
toned landscapes in peasant France
such as Courbet would have
approved of, but learning more from
the open-air technique of Corot. He
soon became aware of the school of
open-air landscape painters centred
on Barbizon (a village near
Fontainebleau), particularly Jean-
François Millet, and slowly began to
lighten his palette, particularly after
he had become intimate with others
of the group which was eventually
to be known as Impressionist. But
even in paintings as late as this one
(1870) there remains a rather stolid,
dour quality about the light and the
way the paint is applied which
recalls the Barbizon school.

Edgar Degas
Jockeys in the rain
1881–6
Pastel on paper
47 × 63.5 cm (18½ × 25 in)
Glasgow: Art Gallery and Museum

About the only outdoor activity that
Degas was normally interested in,
either as a painter or as a person,
was horse-racing. Apparently even
this enthusiasm was very
generalized and theoretical: he seems
not to have been a horseman at all,
and to have taken little interest, as a
spectator or a gambler, in the
mechanics of the sport. Hardly any
of his many works depicting horses
and jockeys (about 45 paintings, 20
pastels, 250 drawings, and 17
sculptures between 1860 and 1900)
are precisely located, or depict
specific horses or riders in
recognisable colours, or show any
part of a race after the 'dead' time
just before the start. Like his ballet-
girls, they are a visual theme
without personal significance.
Jockeys in the rain, an ambitious
pastel dating from either about 1881
or about 1886 (experts differ about
this, and in any case one of the
figures comes from a painting as
early as 1868) is among the most
brilliant, with its variety of poses, its
brilliantly fresh colouring, and the
suggestion of rain made with white
lines, after the manner of Japanese
prints that were greatly admired by
the younger artists in Paris.

Camille Pissarro
The approach to the village of Voisins
1872
Oil on canvas
45 × 55 cm (17¾ × 21⅝ in)
Paris: Louvre

Something of this new quality is already perceptible in this painting of 1872, which has a more distinctly open-air feeling than the compositionally rather similar *Louveciennes road* of two years earlier. In this painting the shifting quality of the pale winter sunlight is vividly captured. But the basic structure of the picture is very solid, with its central roadway narrowing into the distance and its trees almost symmetrically disposed to either side. There is always in Pissarro's paintings a feeling of being close to the soil – the real soil as the peasant knows it and as Courbet knew it – so that whatever changing patterns of light and shade may pass over it, the place itself seems permanent and unchanging. In comparison, the country landscapes of most other Impressionists seem to be the rapid, delighted glimpses of day-trippers – though none the worse for that.

Camille Pissarro
The little bridge at Pontoise
1875
Oil on canvas
65 × 81 cm (25⅝ × 31⅞ in)
Mannheim: Städtische Kunsthalle

One of Pissarro's favourite places for painting during the 1870s was the small town of Pontoise, 30 km (18½ miles) northwest of Paris. He settled there in 1872, and most years he spent part of the summer there, painting the old houses of the town, the farms and orchards round about, the road and rail bridges over the Oise, Viosne, and other rivers, and the neighbouring towns of Osny and Auvers. On some of these painting trips he was accompanied by other Impressionists, notably Cézanne and, later, Gauguin (18 years his junior), whom he had befriended and with whom he often painted side-by-side in the old Impressionist manner. *The little bridge at Pontoise* is one of his earlier works in the vicinity, a painting containing the classic Impressionist motifs of light filtering through leaves and being reflected by water; but it is still careful and stable, rather than seeking to capture the glint and movement of the momentary effect.

C. Pissarro 1875

Camille Pissarro
The Côte des Boeufs at Pontoise
1877
Oil on canvas
114 × 87 cm (44⅞ × 34¼ in)
London: National Gallery

The later 1870s seem to have been for Pissarro a time of personal uncertainty and, in his art, of formal experiment in which he tried out new techniques and approaches, not always very happily. Pissarro was, indeed, always the most impressionable of the Impressionists, tending to take colour from those around him – hence his later wholesale conversion to Divisionism under the influence of Georges Seurat, who was almost 30 years his junior. In 1877 Cézanne came to stay and paint with him at Pontoise, and a number of his paintings from this time seem to show Cézanne's influence – sometimes, as in this work, to triumphant effect. The painting is formally much more

intricate than Pissarro's earlier work, with the farm buildings glimpsed through a screen of trees, the hillside and further trees beyond that, and beyond them the cloudy sky – the kind of elaborately graded recession often found in Cézanne's pictures. Here it gives strength to Pissarro's work without reducing the delicacy with which he renders surfaces and textures.

Claude Monet (1840–1926)
The beach at Trouville
1870
Oil on canvas
38 × 46.5 cm (15 × 18⅜ in)
London: Tate Gallery

Monet's beginnings as a painter were made in his childhood home at Le Havre, where he was encouraged by the great specialist in seashore scenes, Eugène Boudin. He shared to the full the Impressionist taste for painting on the Channel coast of

France, with its constant breezes to give movement to the calmest, sunniest day, its smooth golden sands, and cool grey-blue water. It may have been he who initiated the Impressionist treks to Trouville, Deauville, and other such gracefully fashionable resorts. *The beach at Trouville* is painted in Monet's most sketchy, summary fashion, as though wilfully to provoke the ire of the academics: it really is an 'impression' before all else. But he manages to capture all that he considers important in the picture – primarily the brightness of the sunlight and the way in which, by contrast, the shade of the parasols changes all the colour values and makes the white dress on the left pick up tints reflected from the sand and the chair: what the sensitive eye sees, rather than what the intellect says *ought* to be there.

Claude Monet
Train in the snow
1875
Oil on canvas
69 × 80 cm (27⅛ × 31½ in)
Paris: Musée Marmottan

Throughout his career Monet was particularly fascinated by the effects of fog, mist, steam, and smoke, and was therefore quite happy to paint scenes redolent of the industrial revolution – railway stations full of steam and smoke, and factories and workshops belching out smoke and vapours. It was the purely visual qualities of such scenes which caught his attention: he was making no particular social point; nor did he share the prejudices of many of his contemporaries who wanted to get back to pre-industrial nature, or at least to preserve it unsullied in their paintings, and failed to see the romance and the purely visual excitements of modern life. It is possible that Monet was influenced in this by the work of Turner: he certainly saw Turner's most famous train painting, *Rain, Steam and Speed*, when he came to London to escape the war in 1870. In *Train in the snow* he creates a powerful feeling of romantic melancholy: this could be the train under which Anna Karenina met her death.

Claude Monet
Impression: setting sun (fog)
1872
Oil on canvas
50 × 62 cm (19⅝ × 24½ in)
Paris: Musée Marmottan

In 1872, from his window in Le Havre, Monet painted two views of the harbour, at sunrise and sunset, which were primarily studies in the effect of mist and the light filtering through it. He called them both *Impression*, subtitling one *sunrise* and the other *setting sun (fog)*. It seemed to Monet to be a naturally descriptive title, but when the *sunrise* appeared at the first group show in 1874 the word *Impression* was picked upon and made fun of and became a sort of rallying-point for the painters concerned: from it the term Impressionism was born. Until recently it was supposed that this painting was the one subtitled *sunrise*. But it has been pointed out that it does not correspond to 1874 descriptions of its appearance; and it is now clear that it is in fact the companion piece, *setting sun (fog)*, which was painted at the same time but not shown until the third Impressionist exhibition in 1879.

Pierre-Auguste Renoir
The Moulin de la Galette
1876
Oil on canvas
130 × 175 cm (51½ × 69 in)
Paris: Louvre

The Moulin de la Galette was a
popular open-air dance-hall in
Montmartre, commemorating in its
name a windmill which had long
been a local landmark (see page 61).
Renoir's canvas of that title, done in
1876, is a virtuoso piece of on-the-
spot painting: he took the large

canvas there with the help of a
group of friends, so that he could
paint it all from the life. Three of the
friends – the painters Rivière,
Goéneutte, and Franc-Lamy – are
portrayed sitting at the table on the
right, and others figure among the
dancers. But the work, for all that it
was painted in the open air, is much
too highly finished and cunningly
contrived to be regarded as in any
sense an 'impression'. The
composition, with its several centres
of interest – the conversation at the
table, the dance-floor to the left,

something attracting the attention of
other figures off to the right outside
our range of vision – is brilliantly
bound together by the exquisitely
modulated colour and the
distribution of light and shade by
the favourite Impressionist device of
sunlight dappling through leaves.

Pierre-Auguste Renoir
Sisley and his wife
1868
Oil on canvas
105 × 75 cm (41¾ × 29½ in)
Cologne: Wallraf-Richartz Museum

Renoir, with the face and figure of a
Normandy peasant and his
unaffected working-class manner,
cut a slightly awkward, exotic figure
among the young painters of Paris
when he first arrived there to study.
Much of his early painting has
something of the same
awkwardness: even as late as 1874
Manet told Monet he should advise
Renoir to give up painting, as he
had no talent at all. But little by
little he worked his way towards his
own style, and towards his own

personal contribution to the
Impressionist melting-pot – which
was, above all, an intensely
sensuous response to colour. The
painting of his fellow-Impressionist,
Sisley and his wife, an open-air
portrait, reflects both a touch of
gaucheness (in the slightly
uncomfortable pose) and an
extraordinary colour response (in the
intense reds and greens, and the
almost luminous golden stripes on
the dress). It is one of Renoir's
earliest masterworks.

Pierre-Auguste Renoir
The skiff
1879
Oil on canvas
71 × 92 cm (28 × 36¼ in)
London: private collection

This is one of Renoir's most ecstatically sun-drenched works, a summation in many ways of his period of closest coincidence with the other Impressionists just before they all began to go off in their own distinct directions. It has most of the defining attributes of Impressionism: the large expanse of rippling water, with every colour in the rainbow somehow reflected in the tiny waves and thrown back on to the boats and those in them; the economically sketched greenery of the reeds in the foreground and the lightly indicated woods behind; the girls in the skiff which occupies the centre of the canvas, dressed in white as the Impressionists loved to paint them; and even – a nod, maybe, to Monet – the railway bridge to the right and the train approaching it along the top of the picture, all happily accepted as part of the idyllic scene.

Pierre-Auguste Renoir
Umbrellas
c. 1884
Oil on canvas
180 × 115 cm (71 × 45$\frac{3}{8}$ in)
London: Tate Gallery

Renoir was unashamedly a 'summer person', responding with all the warmth of his temperament to warmth and sunlight around him. But early in the 1880s he developed a new concern with the rendering of form in painting and went through what is known as his 'sour' period, in which he reduced the sensuous colour of his painting and began to depend more on linear elements and on a smoother, drier way of laying on paint. One of the key paintings of this phase is *Umbrellas*, which seems to have been completed around 1884, although there is some evidence that he began it earlier and laid it aside. Certainly the little girls and their mother to the right seem to be painted in a richer, freer style than the rest of the picture, with its chilly slate-grey tones and its unusually rigid composition.

34

Alfred Sisley (1840–99)
Wheatfields near Argenteuil
1873
Oil on canvas
49.5 × 73 cm (19$\frac{1}{2}$ × 28$\frac{3}{4}$ in)
Hamburg: Kunsthalle

This is one of Sisley's least watery
paintings. It is a powerful piece of
design, with the confident upward
sweep of the golden stand of wheat
from the right of the picture, the
green-and-brown cabbage patch in
the centre, and the clump of dark
trees providing the focus of the
whole, and upon which everything
converges. And over all a pale blue
sky with whiffs of white cloud
apparently being blown by the wind
which animates the trees below – an
element of the painting which seems
closer to the practice of Sisley's
English models, especially
Constable, than to anything in the
work of his contemporary French
Impressionists-to-be. Sisley's father,
ruined by the Franco-Prussian War,
had died in 1871, leaving him to
support himself and his family
entirely by painting. The sale of this
painting to Durand-Ruel in 1874,
although for a quite modest price
(his average at this period was
between 200 and 300 francs) was a
step in the right direction.

Alfred Sisley
The footbridge at Argenteuil
1872
Oil on canvas
38 × 60 cm (15 × 23⅝ in)
Paris: Louvre

Sisley was in many respects the most self-effacing and the least deliberately controversial of all the Impressionists, and also the one who stayed closest to the original Impressionist principles throughout his life, painting his quiet country landscapes, more often than not including a river or pond, keeping in touch with his friends, and exhibiting largely through Durand-Ruel, without achieving much commercial success: he is a classic example of the artist who dies destitute and whose prices then immediately rise spectacularly. He was a close associate of the principal figures of Impressionism, having met Monet, Renoir, and Bazille in Charles Gleyre's studio in 1863. But even before that he had discovered for himself the landscapes of Constable and Turner while in England to brush up his English. He had been among the first of the group to discover Argenteuil, and painted this footbridge on one of his early visits.

Alfred Sisley
Regatta at Molesey
1874
Oil on canvas
62 × 92 cm (24$\frac{3}{8}$ × 36$\frac{1}{4}$ in)
Paris: Louvre (Jeu de Paume)

In 1874 Sisley went to England for
four months with his friend and
patron, the singer Jean-Baptiste
Faure. There does not seem to have
been any particular purpose for the
visit: Durand-Ruel had shown
Sisley's work in England in 1872,
and again in 1873 and 1874, but he
was regarded as a new French
painter (in spite of his English
antecedents) and had had no special
success such as might justify a visit
to exploit the English market. But
Faure was rich and paid Sisley's
expenses, and no doubt a change of
scene did not come amiss. At first he
probably stayed with Faure in
Brompton, but his time near the
centre of London is commemorated
by only one painting, a hazy view of
the Thames with St Paul's. Soon he
moved out to the vicinity of
Hampton Court, and worked very
consistently in that area for the next
three months. The *Regatta at
Molesey* dates from this time; it is
one of Sisley's most animated and
joyous works, again dominated by
the feeling of a powerful breeze
which flutters the large flags across
the middle of the composition.

Alfred Sisley
Molesey Weir at Hampton Court
1874
Oil on canvas
50×75 cm ($19\frac{5}{8} \times 29\frac{1}{2}$ in)
Edinburgh: National Gallery of
Scotland

Also from this stay in England
comes *Molesey Weir at Hampton
Court*, one of Sisley's most dynamic
compositions, with the headlong
rush of water from left to right
across the foreground and the high
blue morning sky to suggest that, for
all the presence of bathers to the
extreme left, the weather is more
than a little bracing. It is not known
whether Sisley was in touch with
relatives in England (he retained his
British nationality throughout his
life); such a contact might explain
the otherwise curious choice of
Hampton Court as a base of
operations. He must have been very
comfortable working there: at least
15 paintings from this trip are
known; six of them went into
Faure's collection, probably as some
sort of return for his patronage.

Alfred Sisley
Floods at Port-Marly [right]
1876
Oil on canvas
60×81 cm ($23\frac{5}{8} \times 32$ in)
Paris: Louvre

Sisley's unswerving, unquestioning
acceptance of the Impressionist
doctrine of absolute truth to the
visual impression – plus, of course,
the ability to choose the right
viewpoint so as to make a
satisfactory design – are strikingly
evident in all his finest works. Least
of all the Impressionists does he
seem to have felt the need to
rationalise and philosophise, or to
allow stylistic researches impose
upon his immediate response to
landscape. He touched his high

point in painting in the middle
1870s, and one of his accepted
masterpieces is *Floods at Port-Marly*.
After the exceptionally heavy winter
of 1875 there had been extensive
flooding near Sisley's home at Marly
(west of Paris), and he took the
chance offered by the extraordinary
conjunction of sky and water to
paint a whole series of exquisitely
light, delicate works. (He was
delighted to be able to sell this
painting at once to the collector
Ernest Hoschedé for the modest
price of 180 francs. In 1878
Hoschedé was threatened with
bankruptcy and had to auction his
collection; his 13 Sisleys averaged
112 francs each. In 1900, the year
after Sisley's death, this painting
changed hands for 43,000 francs.)

Alfred Sisley
Misty morning
1874
Oil on canvas
50 × 61 cm (19⅝ × 24 in)
Paris: Louvre

This work is one of Sisley's most remarkable *tours-de-force*. Mist, like snow and even material such as muslin, was often used by Impressionists to demonstrate the way neutral-coloured elements in a painting have the effect of 'absorbing' tones and tints from their surroundings. Obviously the most striking effects could be achieved if the mist was seen to be diffusing strong sunlight or veiling strong-coloured objects. In this painting, however, there is neither strong light nor strong colour. All is reduced virtually to a monotone, the mist merely borrowing faint touches of pink and yellow from the flowers. Yet the effect is infinitely subtle.

Alfred Sisley
Snow at Veneux
1879–82
Oil on canvas
54 × 73 cm (21¼ × 28¾ in)
Paris: Louvre

Although Sisley never appears
consciously to have worried about
whether his style was changing and
developing through the years, his

lack of any perceptible idea about
what he was doing or why meant
that he was more completely
dependent than most on pure
inspiration and the continuing
freshness and immediacy of his
response to the scenes about him.
This might well have been difficult
to sustain at the best of times, but
grinding poverty pushed him to
over-produce, and a certain

heaviness and 'routine' quality is to
be seen in much of his work done
after 1880: the colours became
brighter and coarser, and were
applied with a heavier hand. *Snow at
Veneux* shows the beginning of the
process: although the snow itself
does not permit of bright colours,
the large expanse of wintry sky is
strongly rendered, but lacks entirely
the magic of *Misty morning*.

Paul Cézanne (1839–1906)
The black marble clock
1869–71
Oil on canvas
55 × 74 cm ($21\frac{5}{8}$ × $29\frac{1}{8}$ in)
Athens: Stavros Niarchos Collection

Although Cézanne was one of the Impressionist group almost from his first arrival in Paris, and a member of the Café Guerbois set, as well as exhibiting in the first and third Impressionist shows, it has been argued that he was never really an Impressionist at all. For all that, he did paint alongside other undoubted Impressionists (like Pissarro) on a number of occasions, and shows in many of his paintings of the 1870s the same sort of interest that they had in the play of light over scenes and objects. It can be seen, however, even in a relatively early still-life such as *The black marble clock* that the chief interest for him in the effects of light resided in the way that light and shade define volume and mass. There is something sculpturally monumental about the cup, the clock, the shell, and even the cloth which seems to imply permanence and is far removed from the spontaneous effects sought by the true Impressionists.

Paul Cézanne
A modern Olympia
1870
Oil on canvas
46 × 55 cm (18⅛ × 21⅝ in)
Paris: Louvre

This remarkable painting was Cézanne's main contribution to the first Impressionist show in 1874. If it comes closer to true Impressionism than any other in his oeuvre, it is also by any standards (including Cézanne's) a very strange work indeed. He had painted it four years earlier, in 1870, and it seems to be, among other things, a parody of Manet's famous 1865 Salon nude *Olympia*. That was no doubt rather too staid and conservative for Cézanne's taste, and so here he suggests what the scene might really have been like, with an ungainly curled-up nude apparently having the bed-clothes whipped away from her by a black attendant, while a bearded man who looks suspiciously like Cézanne himself looks on (appreciatively?) in the foreground. Stylistically the picture is exceptional in Cézanne's work, being dashed off in an almost cartoony manner, with very free, fluid brush-strokes and a brilliant palette quite unlike his usual rather severe range of colours.

Paul Cézanne
Madame Cézanne with a fan
1879–82
Oil on canvas
92.5 × 73 cm (36$\frac{1}{2}$ × 28$\frac{3}{4}$ in)
Zürich: E. G. Bührle Collection

In pursuit of his formal researches Cézanne got into the habit of painting the same subjects over and over again, the subject being regarded as the pretext of the painting rather than the essence of it. In this he is more at one with the 'traditional' Impressionists Manet and Degas than with his own closer contemporaries Monet, Renoir, and Sisley. Cézanne painted many self-portraits and many portraits of his wife – presumably because they were the two models most readily to hand. *Madame Cézanne with a fan* was painted in 1879–82 (he was a slow worker, constantly putting paintings aside and working them over and over until he was satisfied; hence the long periods over which many were painted), and is in point of time about halfway through the series. The atmospheric backgrounds of the earlier paintings have given way to a much more severe handling, with the emphasis on the sculptural qualities of the subject and a very dark, subdued colour scheme, although there is still some way to go to the abstract austerity of a decade later.

Paul Gauguin (1848–1903)
Snow, rue Carcel
1883
Oil on canvas
117 × 90 cm (46 × 35$\frac{1}{2}$ in)
Private collection

No one thinks of Gauguin as an Impressionist; but he was a late developer, and at the beginning of his career he was befriended and much encouraged by Pissarro, whom he met in 1877. He was persuaded by Pissarro and Degas to show some sculptures in the fourth Impressionist show (1879), went painting with Pissarro around Pontoise the following year, and exhibited regularly in the remaining four Impressionist exhibitions. His work during this period, strongly influenced by Pissarro, is Impressionist in flavour, and remarkably accomplished; it remains little known largely because Gauguin's style changed radically after the final Impressionist exhibition in 1886. At first glance we would not associate *Snow, rue Carcel* with the specialist in flat patterning and brilliant colouring that Gauguin subsequently became. But the rendering of the cold flat winter light and the faint shadows on the snow already hint at the mastery of his maturity.

Sequels

It is one of life's ironies that in the arts revolutionaries often become back numbers before they have even managed to become the new establishment. Something very like that happened to the Impressionists. During the 12 years spanned by their eight exhibitions, they had acquired a few important patrons, and had won over a few critics, but most of the latter wrote for specialized audiences in small-circulation magazines (the poet Stéphane Mallarmé, who of all the critics at the time understood Impressionism best, was explaining it not to the French but to the English – in the *Art Monthly Review*). The most influential critics, however, were still uncomprehending and hostile, accusing them of not knowing their craft, or merely squirting paint at their canvases, and of being at best madmen, at worst cynical confidence tricksters out to deceive a gullible public. Taking their cue from this, the public determinedly showed that it was not to be taken in: its heart was with the comfortable, story-telling pictures of the Salon, and when it came to the Impressionist exhibitions it was mainly to scoff.

Meanwhile, although the Impressionists continued to present a fairly united front, they were all developing, changing, and in several cases moving away from those very ideals which had brought them together. Degas, always a difficult person to deal with, had from the start gone his own way, having no time at all for the principle of painting on the spot and with immediate truth to nature: he constructed his pictures in the studio as rigorously as any Academic – although of course along very different lines, delighting in curious off-centre compositions derived from the first snapshots and the newly influential Japanese prints. Manet had continued throughout his life to revere and emulate the old masters, often referring back to them for his pictorial concepts, if not for the way he put them on to canvas. And in 1885 Pissarro, seemingly among the quietest and most steadfast of the original Impressionists, underwent a sudden conversion to the ideas of a group of younger painters he had befriended, particularly Georges Seurat, and began painting in the Divisionist style, with paintings composed of thousands of little blobs of pure colour – quite different from anything he had done before.

The changes which had been taking place in the work of Monet, Renoir, and Cézanne were less marked, but were certainly there. Cézanne in particular had always had his own distinct interests and purposes, to such an extent that it has often been questioned whether, even though he exhibited in the first and third group shows and remained friendly with the rest of the Impressionists throughout, he can really be counted as an Impressionist at all. His work, with its growing interest in rendering the volume of things rather than giving a fleeting impression of their effect on the eye, obviously has affinities with the Impressionists in that the effect of volume is created at the outset by the way that light plays on surfaces. But by the early 1880s he had developed away from the sensuous colours of the Impressionists towards a much more austere palette – suggested, no doubt, by the dry landscapes of his native Provence – and had adopted a more economical convention for sketching-in the bare bones of his subjects and for reducing their form to facets rendered in flat patches of subdued colour. It was one of the directions in which art was to go in the years after the last Impressionist exhibition, and Cézanne was to be enormously influential on the generation of major painters who emerged at the turn of the century, leading through Picasso and Braque directly to Analytical Cubism, the first unmistakably 20th-century art movement.

Before that happened, however, there was to be an amazing number of

Camille Pissarro
The Tuileries gardens
1900
Oil on canvas
65 × 92 cm (25⅝ × 36¼ in)
Private collection

In the 1890s Pissarro, after long
years living mainly in the country
around Eragny, began to spend more
and more time in Paris, where he
found new inspiration in the
movement of the city and the

changing effect of the architecture in
different weathers and seasons.
After a brief flirtation with the
Divisionist techniques of Seurat and
Signac in the 1880s he had returned
to his old Impressionist style, but
defined with a new boldness of
effect and using as a rule larger
brush-strokes of pure colour. Not all
his fellow Impressionists approved
of these developments, and although
eventually Pissarro achieved a
measure of financial success (it was

a long time coming) he was not
altogether sure himself about the
quality of his later painting,
suspecting that old age and failing
eyesight were affecting it. When he
painted *The Tuileries gardens* in
1899 he was 69 and working mainly
indoors, from the windows of his
rooms in Paris; but his artistic
energies remained undimmed.

new movements in French art, developing out of or reacting against the theory and practice of the Impressionists. Sometimes it is not clear exactly where they stand. The Divisionists, or Pointillists, are also known as Neo-Impressionists. Indeed, two principals of the movement, Seurat and Signac, exhibited at the eighth Impressionist exhibition alongside the first of Pissarro's paintings influenced by their ideas, and Signac subsequently wrote a book called *From Eugène Delacroix to Neo-Impressionism* (1899), which set out to demonstrate the continuity of French art through the Impressionists. Seurat and Signac believed that they had merely carried Impressionist studies of light and its effects one necessary stage farther, by subjecting it to scientific analysis.

Others who had been connected with Impressionism – mainly through friendship with Pissarro – soon went off in very different directions. Gauguin, for instance, after his Impressionist start (he exhibited at five of the eight group shows) went to paint at Pont-Aven, in Brittany, in 1886, and there evolved a dramatic new style of boldly defined shapes and bright, flat, often arbitrary colours which seemed to deny the very principles of Impressionism. That year he met the young Dutch painter Vincent van Gogh in Paris, and later he became the leader at Pont-Aven of a group of artists preoccupied with mystical essences rather than surfaces. These constituted the first group of what would become generally known as the Post-Impressionists, and in the 1890s they led on (through their mystical interests) to the group known as the Nabis ('prophets'), then to the Intimist painting of Pierre Bonnard and Édouard Vuillard, and (through their use of bold, simple colours) to the Fauves (literally, 'wild beasts') such as Henri Matisse and André Derain.

All the major art movements in France during the 20th century can be seen as deriving, in one way or another, from Impressionism, or at least following on from it by a natural process of influence and reaction. But apart from Bazille and Manet, who had both died relatively young, the founders of Impressionism lived on and continued to work through these periods of violent change in the arts; nor did their art, except for Pissarro's, change radically or all at once. In 1886, at the time of the last group show, they still had many years of active life ahead of them: Sisley died in 1899, Pissarro in 1903, Degas in 1917, Renoir in 1919, and Monet in 1926. It was hardly to be expected that any artist worthy of the name would stand still for so much of his career. Pissarro, who was converted to Divisionism in 1885, began to have doubts about the technique after about four years and looked around for a new way to express his ideas. The problem for him with using an infinitude of tiny dots was that it was so laborious and took the painter farther and farther away from the flickering, fluctuating life of the immediate reality of what he saw, which for any true Impressionist was of central importance. From about 1889 he returned to a broader, simpler version of his Impressionist style, and he adhered to it up to his death. Always the least successful of the Impressionists in worldly terms, Pissarro still managed with Durand-Ruel's help to become commerically established, and his later shows sold well even though he himself and some of his old friends found them disappointing.

Of all the Impressionists, Sisley remained most consistently true to the first ideals of Impressionism, working away quietly at his landscapes with water and snow in a style which deepened but did not change very much through the years. The maverick Degas, who had been very much a man-about-town in early life, gradually became virtually a recluse, posing his models on one floor of his house and then going to paint on another, as notions of immediate truth to direct observation became increasingly irrelevant to him. In his early career he had been rich enough to do just what he liked, but from the early 1880s his fortune was much reduced and the saleability of his pictures became more important. Fortunately for him his art was more approachable to the traditionally minded collector than that of the true Impressionists, mainly because, despite the eccentricities of his compositions, human interest plays a large part in his work (he painted very few pure landscapes), and nobody ever doubted

Claude Monet
Haystack
1891
Oil on canvas
65 × 100 cm ($25\frac{5}{8}$ × $39\frac{3}{8}$ in)
Private collection

During the 1870s Monet had contrived, despite the often parlous state of his finances, to travel quite extensively and paint in many parts of France, as well as in London during his brief exile there. But in 1883 he made a decision which was to influence the whole of his working life from then on. He found a property near the secluded village of Giverny, on the Seine about halfway between Paris and Rouen, and determined to settle there. He lived at Giverny for the rest of his life, and died there in 1926. During the earlier part of his time at Giverny he still travelled, but increasingly he found all the subject-matter for his paintings round about, within easy walking distance of his home, and finally just in his own carefully planned and tended garden. He began in the late 1880s painting systematic series on the same subject: one was of haystacks near his home, and during 1890–1 he painted these in all weathers and at different times of day.

Edgar Degas
After the bath
1888–92
Pastel on paper
104 × 99 cm (41 × 39 in)
London: National Gallery

One of the recurring themes in
Degas's paintings and drawings is
that of women taking a bath, or
getting into or out of one; often the
scene is in a brothel, with a
prostitute washing alone or in the
presence of the client. During the
heyday of Impressionism he had
painted or drawn these subjects in a
rather tight, meticulous technique;
later he worked more and more in
pastel, and his handling of the
medium became looser and looser.
This version of *After the bath*, a
large pastel, seems to have been one
of his more carefully considered
works, since there are several
studies of this particular pose and
two smaller variants. In it we see
the model obviously just out of the
bath, on which she leans with her
right hand while she towels her hair
with her left. The colour is brilliant
and boldly applied in long, separate
strokes of the pastel to indicate very
exactly the modelling of the
woman's back.

that he was a superb draughtsman. His last five years were miserable – his house was demolished and he became blind – but up to that point he continued to make his own way in art, if anything with increased freedom and virtuosity, and carried most of the art world along with him.

Renoir and Monet both survived their stormy youth and controversial middle age to become grand old men of French painting, lionised and able to command high prices for their work. As time went by, Renoir concentrated more and more on painting people rather than landscapes, delighting to paint over and over again his wife and children and in rendering the voluptuous curves of his great peasant nudes. He too had trouble with his eyesight, and in the 1900s his style became broader and broader, his colours more and more garish. Some would see this as a deterioration; others regard his later style as an important progression towards qualities now, after the ascendency of Pop Art, more likely to be highly prized. In the end, crippled by rheumatism and nearly blind, he could work only in sculpture, but in this new medium he produced a number of major works which could not be by anyone else.

Monet, more than any other Impressionist, continued throughout his long life to develop and explore, always within the framework of original Impressionist ideas, but to more and more distant ends. He became absorbed in working on series of paintings which would treat the same subject from the same angle but at different times of day or different seasons of the year, so that he could capture every minute variation in the play of light over, for instance, the façade of Rouen cathedral, or a haystack in the fields near his home at Giverny. In his old age he stayed more and more at home in Giverny, finding all the subjects he needed in the seasonal changes of the plants in his lovingly tended garden, especially the lilies in his lily-ponds. In these last, extraordinary paintings the subject becomes less and less important, until they verge on complete abstraction. And from here, jumping several generations and decades in the history of art, the line of development is clear through to painters like Jackson Pollock and the American Abstract Expressionists of the 1950s and so through to our own day. It is not for nothing that the first Impressionist exhibition of 1874 has been called the birthday of modern art.

Claude Monet
Waterlily pond
1899
Oil on canvas
89 × 93 cm (35 × 36⅝ in)
London: National Gallery

In his last years, when he was old and infirm, Monet seldom set foot outside his garden and painted almost nothing but the lilies in his lily-ponds and the Japanese bridge that arches over them. He had finally bought his property in Giverny in 1890, and in 1893 he bought a further patch of land with a pond and a small stretch of river, over which he built the bridge. From then on his water-gardens were a constant delight to him, and he began painting them over and over again in 1899, which is the date of this *Waterlily pond* with the Japanese bridge. During the next 20 years or so his paintings became more and more abstract, until by the early 1920s many of them consist at first sight of writhing masses and swirls of colour in which specific

features of his garden can be inferred rather than discerned. This shift in style toward abstraction and toward an emphasis on red colours can be attributed partly to the cataracts of the eyes he began to develop in 1908; but after successful eye operations in 1923 he continued to paint in the same style, facing resolutely towards the future.

Claude Monet
Rouen cathedral
1894
Oil on canvas
107 × 73 cm (42¼ × 28¾ in)
Private collection

Another series (1892–4), comparable
to Monet's haystacks, was of the
façade of the cathedral at Rouen,
which lies about 50 km (31 miles)
north-west of Giverny. Again, he
went about it systematically, in full
consciousness that he was painting
a series: all the paintings were done
from the same viewpoint (the
window of a room he rented above a
shop on the Place-de-Rouen) and, as
the light shifted between dawn and
dusk during the winter of 1892–3,
and again a year later, he worked on
the pictures at different moments of
the day and in different weather. In
1895 Durand-Ruel put on a show
featuring 20 of these canvases. The
reactions were very mixed: some
critics approved of the 'weightless'
treatment of the architectural mass,
which makes the building appear as
a screen on to which patterns of
light, creating various harmonies of
colour, could be thrown at random
for the painter's delectation; other
critics were disturbed by the
paintings' seeming lack of any kind
of documentary quality, so that one
had no sense of scale or distance
and no feeling of solidity or volume.

Claude Monet
Waterloo Bridge, London
1901
Oil on canvas
65 × 100 cm (25⅝ × 39⅜ in)
Private collection

A 'feeling of solidity or volume'
was by 1900 about the last thing to
interest Monet in his painting (he
was in this respect the complete
opposite of Cézanne): what
concerned him was not so much the
form of an object as the effect of
light falling upon it – and not light
in general but light at a particular
moment in time. That moment was
to be recorded as it occurred, the
painter's eye instructing his hand,
with as little as possible
intervention by the intellect. Like
other Impressionists Monet was
fascinated by the effects of mist
upon light, so it is not surprising
that he should be drawn back to
London, where vistas of the Thames
were rendered romantically
indeterminate by smoke and fog. In
1899 he began a series of London
views, which by 1904 ran to more
than a hundred, nearly all done from
a balcony of the Savoy hotel. This
iridescent impression of Waterloo
Bridge is a typical example.

Claude Monet
San Giorgio Maggiore, Venice
1908
Oil on canvas
60 × 78.5 cm (23⅝ × 31 in)
Cardiff: National Museum of Wales

Among Monet's farthest travels in
search of new visual stimuli was a
trip to Venice in 1908. While Manet
had been inspired, more than 30
years before, by the crisp, clear air
and brilliant sunlight of the city (see
page 15), Monet's response was
closer to Turner's misty and magical
evocations. In *San Giorgio Maggiore,
Venice* everything is half-glimpsed
through a veil of mist, with the sun
shining through from behind the
church in the centre to blot out even
more effectively any purely
documentary evidence the painting
might vouchsafe about the solid
architecture and the relation of land
to sea. Like his notorious *Impression*
of 1872 (see page 29), this work
might stand as a classic
Impressionist statement – except
that, by this stage in his career,
Monet was not so strict about
working entirely on the spot, and
very likely he sketched this and his
other Venetian subjects on site and
completed them at Giverny.

Pierre-Auguste Renoir
The bathers
1887
Oil on canvas
116 × 170 cm (45¾ × 67 in)
Philadelphia: Museum of Art

Renoir passed quite rapidly through his 'sour' phase (see page 33): a natural buoyancy and love of light and colour soon reasserted itself. But in the gradual parting of the ways which overtook the Impressionists during the mid-1880s he, too, found that he was making his own way in a direction rather different from the rest. The first clear statement of this was in this large composition completed in 1887, the year after the last Impressionist group show. As a result, partly, of his studies of Ingres and the disciplines of classical draughtsmanship, he had arrived at a new style which combined his old love of warm, glowing colour and appreciation of the amply rounded female form with a new crispness of outline and a sharper definition of form. *The bathers* was for him something of an essay in the grand manner, planned and worked on over three years (the principal model being Suzanne Valadon, herself a painter and the mother of Maurice Utrillo, who had been born four years before). When it was exhibited it achieved a large success with the public, although Pissarro disliked a certain arbitrariness and lack of unity in it and only Van Gogh of the Impressionists' later associates wholly approved.

Pierre-Auguste Renoir
Gabrielle with rose
1911
Oil on canvas
55 × 46 cm (27⅝ × 18⅛ in)
Paris: Louvre

From 1890 Renoir, now in his fifties, set enthusiastically about becoming a grand old man of art. He spent increasing amounts of time in the south, where he had first been lured by Cézanne, and the warmth and bright clear sunlight (not to mention the considerable prosperity Durand-Ruel was bringing him at this period) helped him out of a depressive period in his life and what he subsequently recognised had been an impasse in his art. He relaxed, expanded, and took again to painting full-bosomed nudes in the fields or by the rivers, this time with ever richer, lusher brush strokes, so that his paintings seem almost edible. He also painted many flower-pieces and still-lifes, as well as tender and intimate portraits of his wife and children. Gabrielle was a country girl who came to work as a maid in the Renoir household in 1894; being very much Renoir's ideal type of womanhood, she soon became his favourite model as well. *Gabrielle with rose* is typical of his later manner, with its preponderance of warm flesh tints and very liquid handling of the paint, using diluted oils almost like water-colours.

Berthe Morisot (1841–95)
The hydrangea
1894
Oil on canvas
73.5 × 60.5 cm (29 × 23⅞ in)
Paris: Louvre (Jeu de Paume)

Berthe Morisot began as a disciple
of Manet, married his brother, and
was for long the only woman
accepted on equal terms by all the
Impressionists. Her style did not
change spectacularly through the
years, and in many respects she
remained truer to the original ideals
of Impressionism than anyone
except possibly Sisley. *The
hydrangea*, one of her last works, is
a characteristically 'feminine'
subject, showing one girl dressing
another's hair in an intimate
domestic interior, with the
hydrangea in a pot nearby. Most of
Berthe Morisot's paintings were of
women, the models usually from her
immediate family circle.

Paul Cézanne
Mont Sainte-Victoire with tall pine
1886–7
Oil on canvas
60 × 73 cm (23⅝ × 28¾ in)
Washington: Phillips Collection

Even during the period of the
Impressionist shows, Cézanne, a
Provençal by birth and upbringing,
rarely stayed in the north for long at
a time. After 1886, when he
inherited his father's estate near
Aix-en-Provence, he remained more
and more in the south. From his
family house he could see Mont
Sainte-Victoire, which was to be an
obsessive theme in Cézanne's
painting for the rest of his life. He
painted it constantly, from every
possible angle, but usually from a
distance, and frequently with some
sort of framing device, as in this
version, where the tree trunks and
leafy branches accentuate the depth
of the field of vision.

Paul Cézanne
Boy in a red waistcoat
1890–5
Oil on canvas
79.5 × 64 cm (31⅜ × 25¼ in)
Zürich: E. G. Bührle Collection

Cézanne was the most intellectual of all the artists connected with Impressionism, and his art has the clearest and most explicit philosophical base. He thought extensively and deeply about the need to reconcile perceived reality with an inner sense of order and design. It was part of his deepest belief that there was in fact an underlying order and design in all of nature, and that the prime task of the painter was to discover and display it. If he could contrive to see deeply enough beneath the surface to the true essence of things, a deliberate reconciliation should not be necessary because there was, at the deepest level, only harmony. It was in search of this harmony that

Cézanne would sometimes happily countenance superficial distortion. In this version of *Boy in a red waistcoat* – one of a series of an Italian model which constitute his most relaxed, graceful, and richly coloured later work – he deliberately extended the right arm for purposes of harmonious design, to the dismay and disgust of uncomprehending contemporary critics.

Paul Cézanne
The large bathers
1904–5
Oil on canvas
130 × 195 cm (51¼ × 76¾ in)
London: National Gallery

Another constant theme throughout
Cézanne's art was that of bathers,
male and female, usually grouped in
a woodland setting by the edge of a
stream or pool. Some of the earliest,
dating from the early 1870s, seem to
have mythological overtones and are
related to paintings he was doing

around the same time on the
temptation of St Anthony and on
Bathsheba. They soon cut free from
such academically respectable
reference, and in the 1880s he
painted a number of large canvases
exploring the purely formal
relationships between figures and
landscape. (At about the same time
Renoir was doing the same thing, in
a wholly different way, with his
large *Bathers* – see pages 52–3). After
1900 Cézanne again reverted to the
subject, this time treating it in a
much more baroque manner and

reducing the detail of figures and
background to the minimum. In
1904–5 he completed several
versions of the *Large bathers* (the
title refers to the size of the painting,
not of the figures), and in this version
he carries his abstracting tendency
to its ultimate extreme.

Paul Gauguin
The vision after the sermon
1888
Oil on canvas
73 × 92 cm (28¾ × 36¼ in)
Edinburgh: National Gallery of
Scotland

During the period in which he was
close to Pissarro, Gauguin had been
a true believer in all the principles
of Impressionism, at least as
Pissarro practised them. But soon
after the final Impressionist
exhibition and Pissarro's radical
(if temporary) conversion to
Divisionism, Gauguin underwent a
kind of almost mystical revelation,
and his art was transformed out of
all recognition. He himself had a
very brief flirtation with Divisionism,
but meanwhile he was thinking
about synthesis in art, and how to
express ideas without going back to
old-fashioned story-telling in
painting. Then, on his first visit to
Brittany in 1886, it all began to come
together in the shape of a quasi-
symbolic set of relationships
between lines, colours, and ideas. By
1888, when *The vision after the
sermon* was painted, he had found
his true voice at last (he was then
just 40) and had become the leader
of a group of mystical painters
centred on the village of Pont-Aven
in Brittany. Henceforth his work
was strange and splendid and
richly, unrealistically coloured – and
could hardly have been farther from
Impressionism.

Vincent van Gogh (1853–90)
The Moulin de la Galette
1886
Oil on canvas
46 × 38 cm (18 × 15 in)
Glasgow: Art Gallery and Museum

At the time he painted *The vision* (1888) Gauguin was allied with the young Dutch painter who was to be the other leading figure in Post-Impressionism. Vincent van Gogh had come to Paris in 1886 after studying in Holland with his cousin Anton Mauve, a Dutch equivalent of the Barbizon painters. He soon managed to meet a lot of painters of his own generation, and flirted very briefly with Impressionism before finding his own style, with the help and encouragement of Gauguin. *The Moulin de la Galette* is one of his few paintings in which the Impressionist influence can be felt – particularly the rather drab, sober style Pissarro had affected until shortly before. It shows the windmill, in the still-rural part of Paris around Montmartre, which had given its name to the dance-hall in Renoir's painting (page 30). At about this time Pissarro began to explain to him the new Divisionist theories of colour; Van Gogh henceforward adopted a much more brilliant palette, and began to apply paint first in the little dots of the Divisionists, then in larger blobs in a manner that was wholly his own. He had only four years of highly personal painting ahead of him before his suicide in July 1890.

Henri de Toulouse-Lautrec
(1864–1901)
Portrait of Jeanne Wenz
1886
Oil on canvas
80 × 58 cm (31½ × 22⅞ in)
Chicago: Art Institute

Another complete outsider who was touched for a brief moment by Impressionism was Henri de Toulouse-Lautrec. He was something of a juvenile prodigy, painting very competent pictures of horses and riders and retainers on and around his aristocratic family's estates even before he began his formal studies at the age of 14. On the fringes of the Paris art world before 1880, he must have been aware of the Impressionists, even though his own training was entirely conservative and academic. When he was 18 he painted a charming open-air portrait of his mother which seems to show Impressionist influences, and by his early twenties he was beginning (under the artistic influence, no doubt, of Degas) to explore the cafés and music halls of Paris and to haunt the wings of theatres in search of subject-matter. The *Portrait of Jeanne Wenz* is a sober, carefully composed piece such as Renoir might have painted in his 'sour' period; it gives little hint of the mature Lautrec, with his dazzling colour and his wicked sense of the grotesque, who was to emerge all at once the following year (1887) with his own bizarre observations on the Cirque Fernando.

Georges Seurat (1859–91)
The Île de la Grande Jatte
1884–6
Oil on canvas
64.7 × 81.2 cm (25½ × 32 in)
New York: Whitney Collection

The last Impressionist group show in 1886 was clearly the end of something, but it was also decidedly a beginning. The 'classic' phase of Impressionism was over, along with any apparent unity of style or purpose among the original leaders. But Pissarro, always the most fatherly and sympathetic of the group towards younger men, had 'discovered' and brought in two new painters, Georges Seurat and Paul Signac, then 26 and 22 years old respectively. Seurat had devoted a good deal of time to the study of Michel-Eugène Chevreul's theories of colour, and he worked out his own system of creating colour in painting by exploiting the way in which tiny dots of pure colours, when viewed from a distance, are synthesised by the eye. He converted Pissarro to his notions, and Pissarro then converted Signac. All three, and Pissarro's son Lucien, showed Divisionist paintings at the 1886 show. The big sensation was Seurat's monumental *Sunday afternoon on the Île de la Grande Jatte*, in the large version with statuesque figures; this smaller version of the same view but without the figures was painted at the same time. In face of such bold and confident innovations, Impressionism itself seemed suddenly quite tame and conventional. Its day was over: the Post-Impressionist era had dawned.

Index

Acknowledgements
The publishers thank the following
organizations and individuals for their
kind permission to reproduce the
photographs in this book:
Ashmolean Museum, Oxford 44–5;
Bayerische Staatsgemäldesammlungen,
Munich (Cooper-Bridgeman Library) 14;
Bührle Foundation, Zürich (Cooper-
Bridgeman Library) 43 left, 56 left;
Chicago Art Institute, U.S.A. (Cooper-
Bridgeman Library) 2–3; By Courtesy of
Christie's (Cooper-Bridgeman Library)
50, 51 above; Cooper-Bridgeman
Library 7, 15 below, 60, (Phaidon
Archive) endpapers and 32–3, 47
below; Courtauld Institute Galleries,
London (Cooper-Bridgeman Library) 1,
16–17; Glasgow Art Gallery (Cooper-
Bridgeman Library) 23 right, 61;
Hamburg Kunsthalle (Cooper-
Bridgeman Library) 15 above, (Ralph
Kleinhempel) 34; Kaier Collection,
Copenhagen (Cooper-Bridgeman
Library) 43 right; Musée du Louvre,
Paris/Jeu de Paume (Cooper-Bridgeman
Library) 10–11, back jacket and 19,
22–3, 24 left, 34–5, 36–7, 39 above and
below, 40–1, 42, 53 right, 54 left; Musée
Marmottan, Paris (Cooper-Bridgeman
Library) 28–9, 29 left; By Courtesy of the
Trustees, The National Gallery, London
26, 27, (Cooper-Bridgeman Library) 13,
20 left, 20–1, 33 right, 47 above, 48–9,
56–7; National Gallery of Scotland,
Edinburgh (Cooper-Bridgeman Library)
38, 58–9; National Gallery of Wales,
Cardiff (Cooper-Bridgeman Library) 51
below; Nationalmuseum, Stockholm 11
left; Stavros Niarchos Collection, Paris
(Cooper-Bridgeman Library) 41 right;
Philadelphia Museum of Art, U.S.A.
(Cooper-Bridgeman Library) 52–3;
Phillips Collection, Washington, D.C.
(Cooper-Bridgeman Library) front
jacket, 54–5; private collection (Cooper-
Bridgeman Library) 8–9, 18; Wallraf-
Kunsthalle, Mannheim (Cooper-
Bridgeman Library) 24–5; Victoria and
Albert Museum, London (Cooper-
Bridgeman Library) 8–9, 18; Wallraff-
Richartz Museum, Cologne 31 left; John
Hay Whitney Collection, New York
(Cooper-Bridgeman Library) 30–1, 62–3.
The paintings reproduced on the
following pages are © S.P.A.D.E.M.,
Paris 1981: front cover, 1, 19 and back
cover, 20 left, 20–1, 23 right, 28–9, 29
left, 30–1, 32–3, 33 right, 47 above and
below, 48–9, 50, 51 above and below,
52–3, 53 right.